Daily Habits of Successful People

How to Steal Successful People Habits

Copyright © 2022

All rights reserved.

DEDICATION

The author and publisher have provided this e-book to you for your personal use only. You may not make this e-book publicly available in any way. Copyright infringement is against the law. If you believe the copy of this e-book you are reading infringes on the author's copyright, please notify the publisher at: https://us.macmillan.com/piracy

1 - They Start the Day Early

One of the core habits of successful people is that they get out of bed early. It provides them a sense of confidence to plan things ahead so that they can easily accomplish their daily tasks. They make use of this time by involving in exercise and planning the activities of the entire day.

There are many outstanding benefits of getting up early. That's why CEO's of top companies make a habit of waking up early in the morning.

2 - They Give Value to Meditation

Meditation has many physical and mental benefits like

it removes stress, controls anxiety, boosts self-awareness, etc. Many people, who achieve success in life, have discovered uncountable benefits of meditation. They are used to meditate every day because it improves their memory, along with offering many other benefits associated to it.

3 - They Love to Read

Do you know that reading routine can boost your smartness?

According to a study conducted by Emory University, neuroscientists discovered that reading a single novel improves brain function.

It is one of the most common habits of successful persons. Most, if not all, of the successful people have the habit of reading. Reading helps them think better and learn something new everyday. It is hard to disagree that learning something new everyday definitely makes you better.

4 - They Spend Time on Focused Thinking

Focused thinking is the most alerted state of your mind because it allows your brain to concentrate at its best by removing all the distractions.

Most of the successful people have a regular habit of focused thinking for around 30 minutes during which they think regarding all the essential aspects like health, relationship, business, etc. so that they can analyze everything in a better way and may come up with a better strategy to accomplish things.

According to Duke Medical School's Imke Kirste, silence is linked with the development of new cells in the area of the brain that is responsible for learning and memory. So, by practicing focused thinking, you can discover better solutions because your mind feels less stress at that time.

5 - They Exercise Daily

How can you become successful if you have no plan

for dealing with stress?

According to the Anxiety and Depression Association of America, seventy percent of adults are a victim of stress in the U.S.

This is one of the major reasons why successful people make a habit of exercise on a daily because they know that if they remain in stress all the time, then they can't deliver their best.

Doing exercise on a daily basis or at least four to five times a week not only help them enhance their memory and mental sharpness but also enable them to increase their creativity.

6 - They Network with Similar People

Living around successful people have a huge impact on your own success because they keep you motivated. That's why successful people prefer to develop relationships among positive and motivated people so that they can have the company of the right people. They try their best to limit their exposure among negative people because they believe that it can create a negative impact on their personality.

7 - They Are Goal-Oriented

Setting goals is a nice habit as it increases your dedication at work and provides more clarity in making decisions. Almost every successful person likes to set short term goals because they know that creating the short term goals and achieving them with success will help them come closer to the bigger, long term goal.

8 - They Chase their Goals Themselves

Successful people believe in the philosophy of being your own boss because it helps them get the professional freedom instead of working 9 to 5 chasing other people dreams.

Successful people don't waste their time fulfilling the dreams of others. They make their own goals and work hard to get them because if they spend time living the dream of others, then they can't achieve what they have planned to achieved in their own lives.

9 - They set High Self-Standard

As far as self-standard is concerned, everyone has the right to choose. But, successful people don't compromise on self-standard. They set a high self-standard because it helps them produce great commitment, momentum, and results which are essential for success.

10 - They Take Sufficient Sleep

Having enough sleep is essential for being successful in life. It not only sharpens your brain but also helps to boost your mood.

Successful people know the importance of adequate sleep that's why they prefer to take a sufficient amount of sleep daily so that they can set themselves up for the top quality work.

11 - They Don't Rely On Single Source of Income

Successful people always work towards creating multiple income streams because they know that relying completely on a single source of income can never provide them the financial stability.

They normally have around three to five income streams so that they don't have to waste too much time dealing with the financial crisis.

12 - They Avoid Things That Waste Time

For every successful person, time is money. They are used to spend their time wisely because they know that every day they have a specific amount of time that needs to be spent effectively for being successful.

Instead of wasting time scrolling Facebook, watching Netflix, etc. they prefer to utilize time on things that make them more productive.

13 - They Maintain Their Daily Task Record

Getting things done on time is important to become successful, that's why most of the successful people have a habit of keeping their activities in a specific journal or software so that they can track their daily achievements. It helps them stay in touch with all of their essential tasks that are extremely necessary to get done.

14 - They Start the Day with Small Meaningful Tasks

One of the best way using which successful people

handle all their daily tasks is that they categorize them from small to big. When they start their day and get some of their meaningful tasks done, then it provides them extra motivation and increases their self-confidence to handle other bigger and complex tasks effortlessly.

15 - They Consider Problems as Gifts

A lot of people usually give up when they encounter problems because they don't have the capability to deal with these problems. But successful people have a different story; they consider these problems as an opportunity to improve and learn lessons from these troubles to avoid them in the future.

16 - They Take Care of Their Health

Successful people believe that a healthy body makes a healthy mind. They know that they can't sacrifice their health by eating unhealthy food because it keeps them away from the road of success. They eat a well-balanced diet so that they remain fit and energetic and accomplish whatever they want.

17 - They Take Instant Actions

Planning things and setting priorities is great, but they

become useless if you don't take appropriate action at the the right time or come up with reasons for not acting in accordance to the situation.

Successful people don't take too much time making decisions as compared to other people because they know that it's one the key elements that helps towards your success.

18 - They Show Positive Attitude

Positive attitude not only helps to enhance trust in your capabilities but also ensures that you achieve your goals successfully.

According to successful people, positive attitude is the

main cause of their success because it gives them enough strength to overcome difficult situations and not to give up.

19 - They are People Oriented

Good relationship with other people matters a lot to the successful people because they know that real happiness in life comes with how well you behave with others.

They work a lot in increasing patience, compassion, and kindness because they understand that it will make them a wonderful human being, which is important for success.

20 - They Accept Failure and Start Again

Successful people never live in the past because they have a different mindset. They try new things, make mistakes, and learn from them. This attitude is something which is not common among other people because they have a lot of fear of failure, which keeps them away from experimenting with new things.

21 - They Create an Ideal Daily Routine

Having a perfect daily routine is necessary for a successful life because it's not only about creating an ideal morning plan and forget about the entire day.

Successful people give importance to create an impeccable routine for the entire 24 hours by fixing their time slots and accommodating fixed time to all the tasks based on priorities.

22 - They Stick to Their Routines

Creating a successful daily routine is not enough if you don't follow it. Highly successful people not only invest time in creating these routines but also gives equal importance when it comes to following these routines. They know that these routines will not only structure their lives but also save their time and make them more efficient.

23 - They Like to Take Risks

In order to achieve extraordinary things in your life, it is necessary to take calculated risks because if you are too scared to try new things out, then accomplishing great things in life can just be a dream for you.

Successful people never fear taking risks because they know that it will make their life more rewarding by providing them with various opportunities.

24 - They Pay Attention to Details

Paying attention to details can make things so much

better in terms of accuracy, time and quality. Many people ignore to pay attention to details, which cost them time and money. But, successful people are tend to pay the due attention to this quality because they don't want to repeat a single task again and again and waste their valuable time and money.

25 - They Show Confidence in Their Abilities

Confidence is essential for having a positive mental attitude. It not only helps to improve your performance but also enables you to feel more relaxed in social settings.

Successful people believe in their abilities way before

they get success. This level of confidence helps them get bigger targets in life with ease.

26 - They Manage Their Emotions Smartly

Mental strength plays a major role in self-improvement because it helps you to transform the challenges into opportunities so that you can enjoy great satisfaction in life.

Successful people are mentally strong. They clearly know what influence their emotions have on their behaviors and thoughts the entire day.

27 - They Are Good Communicators

Excellent communication skill is undoubtedly a major skill if you want to get listed in the list of highly successful people. It not only helps you to understand the perspective of others but also enables you to be understood easily.

Highly successful people are well aware of the benefits of having great communication skill. They work on this skill continuously to get better with time.

28 - They Practice Self Control

Self-control has the power to improve your focus and decision-making capability. It has a huge impact on success, which successful people knows very well. Most of them try to spend limited time on the things that are tempting but do not contribute positively to their success. It is because it makes the entire process of self-control stress-free for them.

29 - They Value Solitude

Solitude brings you the opportunity to discover yourself because it creates an atmosphere of deep thinking. Successful people like to spend some time in solace because they know that it will provide them the possible way to work through their problems and increase their productivity at work.

30 - They Are Conscientious

Being conscientious can bring many positive changes in your life. It helps to get more satisfaction at work and allows you to take care of your health to live a better life.

Successful people like to be conscientious because it enables them to set and achieve goals while facing every hardest obstacle of life.

31 - They keep Balance in Life

Having a well-balanced life is necessary for your health

and well-being in this modern world. It not only improves your mood but also helps to reduce stress.

Successful people keep a perfect balance between work and life because they know that it's necessary to take some time out from their busy life and get back with more power and energy.

32 - They Deprioritize All Useless Opportunities

When you create your goals, there are many tasks that don't add a lot to your main goal. The best way to deal with them is to deprioritize from your list, which successful people do because they know consuming time on unnecessary tasks will keep them away from attaining their goals.

33 - They Always Look For Solution

Many people have a habit of making arguments and finding unnecessary reasons if they are unable to get what they want to achieve. But, the story is different with successful people. They work extremely hard to find the right solution to the problem even if it looks impossible to others.

34 - They Don't Play the Blame Game

It's easy to blame others for all the problems instead of

taking responsibilities for the outcomes. Successful people don't involve in the blame game because they know that it's simply a waste of time. Rather than blaming other people, they accept their mistakes and learn lesson from them to avoid them repeating next time to their life.

35 - They Appreciate Continuous Learning

Continuous learning is an excellent approach to discover new ways of dealing with things. It helps to prepare you for all the unexpected changes in your life by acquiring new skills.

Successful people believe that learning is all about

growing. That's why they spend sufficient time learning new things to become more productive.

36 - They Face Bad Day with Courage

It's not possible to score successes every single day. Sometimes, you hit your targets and sometimes, you miss them. How do take these missed targets matter the most, because it is the attitude that can help you take over massive hurdles.

Successful people don't stop everything on the basis of having a bad day. They believe that it's a part of life and start things with more energy and motivation from the next day.

37 - They Accept Challenges

Challenges are the part of everyone's life, but overcoming them normal in the life of a successful person because they know that things never remain the same as they planned. But, because they accept challenges, that's why they have all the courage to deal with unexpected situations and achieve unexpected things which other people can't achieve.

38 - They like to Live Outside Comfort Zones

Many people love to live inside their comfort zone, which let them miss so many opportunities in life. But, successful people don't prefer to live inside the comfort zone. They challenge themselves so that they can reach the peak of their performance and deliver their best.

39 - They know Money Is Not Everything

Some people believe that success is all about money. They put all their effort into finding ways to become rich, believing that it will make them a highly successful person in life. But, successful people know that only getting rich is not a success because there are many other things that contribute to a successful life.

40 - They Avoid Laziness

Laziness kills productivity. That's why successful people never get lazy and do their best to finish things on time or even before time. But, that doesn't mean that they don't take any relaxation in life. They enjoy time with their friends and family but remain active and work smartly when required.

41 - They Give Importance to Feedback

Feedback can be positive or negative, but how one reacts to them define their potential for success. Successful people are open to constructive criticism because they believe that it provides them with an opportunity to improve in their life rather other people who react quite negatively to the feedback's.

42 - They Don't Look For Shortcuts

Many people look for a quick fix of success, which is not the right way because success doesn't come overnight. It needs smart work and patience to let the success knock your door.

Successful people don't search for shortcuts. They put all the efforts and hard work that is required to make them successful.

43 - They Start with the End in Mind

Successful people never create goals without keeping the end in mind because they believe that it's necessary to keep the bigger picture in mind while creating goals. It provides them a clear vision regarding their destination so that they can work towards them with more motivation.

44 - They Practice What They Say

Many people have a habit of delivering remarkable speeches in front of other people, but they don't even follow themselves what they say. But, successful people don't behave like that because they become a role model by actively doing the things which they promote among other people.

45 - They Maximize their Strength

One big reason that makes a person successful from others is by maximizing its strength. Instead of utilizing time on too many things, they concentrate on the things in which they are good at because they know that it will help them achieve success more smoothly.

46 - They Visualize Success

Visualization gives a person the power and courage to

tackle daunting tasks as it triggers the hormones that make the process of attaining goals easier. Successful people visualize success long before getting it. It increases positive thoughts in them and helps them optimize their performance to the top.

47 - They don't wait for Right Time

A lot of people have a habit of waiting for the right time to act, which is simply a lame excuse because it is never a perfect time. Successful people know it very well. That's why they don't wait too much and take the bold step of doing things rather than waiting for the perfect time.

48 - They Make Their Own Luck

There is a common concept of good luck and bad luck among people. When things go to their favor, they consider it their good luck and when things go against them, they consider it their bad luck.

Successful people don't believe in the concept of good luck and bad luck. They create their luck by putting all the hard work.

49 - They Show More Humility

Humility is one thing which is quite common around successful people. They accept their mistakes easily and happily because they have the courage to correct them without making arguments. They don't have issues learning from others because they believe that it helps them become more successful in life.

50 - They Never Complain

When things go out of hand, people normally start complaining instead of finding the solution. Successful people know that complaining is all about wasting their time and energy. Rather than wasting time complaining, they work on getting the solution to their problem.

51 - Measure Success in Happiness Rather than Wealth

The modern generation of employees are increasingly motivated by factors other than wealth, with job satisfaction, benefits and empowerment all key considerations. This also represents a shift in the way that people measure their success, as defining it in pounds and pence or dollars and cents only leads you to consistently chase a higher amount with ever achieving true satisfaction. This can be counter-productive, so be sure to create a clearly defined vision of success and understand precisely what it means to you.

52 - Challenge yourself and Do Hard Things

You cannot succeed in life without first achieving personal growth, which demands a willingness to accept and overcome difficult challenges. It is only though overcoming obstacles that we are able to learn and develop critical life skills, and it is these attributes that will equip us to obtain success. By challenging yourself and confronting difficult tasks, you can also change your mind-set with regards to the possibilities that life holds.

53- Listen to Constructive Criticism and the Opinion of Others

While positive feedback can improve your morale and motivate you to achieve success, it is your ability to respond to constructive criticism that will ultimately empower you to reach your goals. After all, this type of feedback highlights areas in which you need to improve, rather than simply reaffirming your strengths as an individual. Your weaknesses can then be targeted through training and development, which in turn will empower you as a stronger and more rounded individual.

54 - Work harder than your Competition and Those Around you

While you can only control your own efforts in the pursuit of your goals, it is important to remember that each individual's success is also determined by those around them. When competing with others for a specific goal or prize, for example, you must do everything within your power and leave no stone unturned if you attain success. At the heart of this is your level of dedication to the cause, as making a commitment to work harder than those around will ultimately afford you a critical edge.

55 - Make Complacency Your Enemy

One of the biggest obstacles to long-term success is complacency, which can easily set-in after positive feedback or the attainment of short-term goals. You must strive to use these achievements as a springboard, however, and rededicate yourself to the cause with renewed vigor. Take the example of footballer Cristiano Ronaldo, who despite emerging as one of the best players in the world continues to commit himself to a punishing daily fitness regime that encourages self-improvement.

www.ingramcontent.com/pod-product-compliance
Lightning Source LLC
Chambersburg PA
CBHW070140230526
45472CB00004B/1620